Dried Delight

10½"x5"x4" chipwood strawberry basket
four 1¼" wide dried mini lotus pods
nine 12" long dried mini cattails
1 oz. of dried nigella
1 oz. of dried dark red cockscomb
1 oz. of dried wheat celosia
1 oz. of dried avena or oats
2 oz. of dried wheat or barley
seven 1½" wide mauve dried strawflowers
1 oz. of dried baby everlasting flowers
six 24" lengths of raffia
1 oz. of Spanish moss
U-shaped floral pins
4"x4"x8" block of floral foam for drieds
basic supplies (see inside the front cover)

1 Cut foam to fit the basket and glue in place. Cover the foam with moss and secure with U-shaped floral pins. Cut one strawflower to 2" and two to 1"; glue them in a triangle at the right front corner of the basket. Glue four lotus pods to the left of the strawflowers.

2 Break the cockscomb into 1"–2" wide clumps. Glue three 2" clusters behind the strawflowers and pods with the strawflowers nestling under the cockscomb. Glue a 1" cluster of the cockscomb to the left of the pods and glue the remaining small pieces between the pods and the front of the basket. Cut the cattails to 5"–11" lengths and insert into the left back corner of the basket. Cut the wheat into 4"–11½" lengths and glue throughout the cattails.

3 Cut the celosia into 3"–5" sprigs; insert the longer pieces into the back left of the arrangement. Insert the remaining celosia to the front and to the right of the wheat angling it outward. Cut the avena to 6"–11". Insert the longer sprigs into the left back foam; insert the shorter sprigs in front of and to the right of the wheat.

4 Cut three nigella stems to 2" and insert into the foam center. Cut the remaining nigella into 3"–7" sprigs and insert them in a cluster in the center of the basket. Cut four strawflowers to 1" and glue into the left front of the basket. Separate the baby everlasting into 1"–2" clusters and glue among the strawflowers and nigella as shown. Hold all the raffia together and make a shoestring bow (see inside the back cover) with 2" loops and 4" tails. Use your thumbnail to shred the raffia into thin strands. Glue the bow to the front basket rim as shown in the large photo.

Country Garden

18" grapevine wreath

1⅞ yards of 2½" wide peach/cream plaid ribbon

6¼"x8" gray-blue wood gate

1¾"x3" "Bloom Where You Are Planted" sign

2¾"x3¼" wood birdhouse

one 1½"x2¼" gathering basket

1 oz. of dried German statice

1 oz. of dried mini gypsophila

1 ivy bush with four 6" long branches of many 2"–3"
  long leaves

2 stems of peach silk zinnias, each with a
  2", a 2½", and a 3" wide blossom

1 stem of peach silk tweedia with twenty 1½" wide
  blossoms

1 stem of dark peach silk tweedia with nine 2" wide
  blossoms

two 22" lengths of raffia

1" ball of Spanish moss

1 oz. of green sheet moss

basic supplies (see inside the front cover)

1 Glue the gate to the inside bottom of the wreath. Glue sheet moss across the wreath bottom, covering the left lower edge of the gate and 4" up the right side. Glue the basket as shown.

2 Glue the sign to the top right corner of the gate. Use the ribbon to make an oblong bow (see inside the back cover) with a center loop, two 3½" loops, four 4" loops and 7" tails. Glue at 7:00. Glue the birdhouse at 11:00. Hold the raffia strands together and tie into a shoestring bow with 2" loops and tails; shred the loops and tails with your thumbnail and glue to the top front of the birdhouse. Cut the ivy branches from the main stem. Glue a small tuft of Spanish moss into the birdhouse opening. Glue an ivy branch at 8:00 and one at 9:00, both climbing up the left side of the wreath. Glue the third extending downward from below the bow; glue the last ivy branch on the right side of the wreath extending downward from 1:00.

3 Cut a 3" zinnia to 2" and glue it to the wreath at 1:00. Cut the other 3" zinnia to 6" and glue just above the bow, bending the stem so the blossom faces forward. Cut the 2½" blossoms to 6"; glue one to the left of the 3" blossom and one to the right, curving as shown. Cut the 2" blossoms to 6" and glue one above each 2" blossom as shown.

4 Cut all the tweedia into 4" sprigs and glue in 2–4 blossom clusters among the zinnias and ivy as shown. Cut two 2½" sprigs each of statice and gypsophila and glue into the basket. Cut the rest into 4" sprigs; glue evenly spaced among the flowers and ivy as shown in the large photo. Make a wire hanger (see inside the front cover) on the back of the wreath.

Watering Can Bouquet

9"x5" wooden watering can with a 6" spout and
a 4" handle

1 stem of yellow silk yarrow with two 9"–11"
and three 5"–6" sprigs, each with a 2½" wide
blossom cluster

1 bush of white silk daisies with nine 9" long
branches of four 2"–2½" blossoms and one
bud

2 stems of silk dusty miller, each with three
6"–8" long sprigs and ten 2"–3" leaves

1 stem of yellow silk phlox with three 9" sprigs
of 1½"–1¾" wide blossoms and four buds

2 stems of white silk alstroemeria, each with two
12"–14" sprigs of four 2½" wide blossoms
and three buds

1 stem of white silk euphorbia with many clusters of three ½" wide blossoms and many
¾"–1¼" long leaves

six 6" green silk leaf stems each with three
2"–3" long leaves

1 curly rattan spray with twenty 13" lengths of
dried rattan

1 oz. of dried mini gypsophila

Sixteen 30" lengths of raffia

1 oz. of Spanish moss

4"x4"x8" block of floral foam for drieds

U-shaped floral pins

basic supplies (see inside the front cover)

1 Cut foam to fit the watering can and glue in
place. Cover the foam with moss and secure with
U-shaped floral pins. Cut one phlox sprig to 9" and
one to 5". Attach each to a pick (see inside the front
cover). Glue the 9" sprig near the spout and the 5"
sprig near the handle, both extending outwards. Cut
the rest of the stem to 14" and glue it into the center.

2 Cut each alstroemeria to 13" and remove the
lower 4" of leaves. Glue one on each side of the
center phlox. Cut the sprigs off the yarrow stem and
attach each to a pick making them 9"–11" long. Insert
the 9"–11" sprigs 2" apart in the center of the foam,
angling slightly outward. Glue a 6" sprig into the back
of the arrangement near the spout as shown. Glue the
remaining sprigs into the front near the spout as
shown in the large photo. Cut the daisies to 7"–12"
sprigs and insert throughout the arrangement.

3 Cut the rattan lengths off the spray and wire to a
pick in clusters of four; insert the picks evenly
spaced throughout the arrangement. Cut a 10" euphorbia sprig and insert it near the handle curving it around
the handle. Cut the remaining euphorbia into 3"–6"
sprigs and glue around the watrering can rim extending over the edge.

4 Insert 6"–12" sprigs of gypsophila evenly spaced
throughout the arrangement. Cut the leaves from
the leaf stems and glue evenly spaced around the edge
of the can. Use 16 strands of raffia to make a shoestring bow (see inside back cover) with 2" loops and
8" tails; glue it to the top of the handle.

back view

handle side view

9"x17" twig arch trellis
2 oz. of pink mini dried rosebuds
36" rose garland with many mauve rosebuds,
    ½"–¾" leaves and ¾" wide open roses
1 oz. of pink dried mini gypsophila
1 oz. of dried German statice
1½"x2" terra cotta pot
2"x2¼" wooden birdhouse
acrylic paints: mauve, gray, dark brown
#4 flat paintbrush
½ oz. of sheet moss
3" of ¹⁄₁₆" wide dowel
two 1" Styrofoam® balls
oval 2¼" wide wooden "Bed & Breakfast" sign
    painted white and yellow with wire hanger
tweezers or toothpicks
basic supplies (see inside the front cover)

¾"

1 Shape the garland and wire it to climb up and over the arch as shown, leaving 5" at the lower right bare.

2 Paint the birdhouse mauve and the roof gray; glue it to the upper arch at the left. Glue the sign to the center of the upper bar on the arch.

3 Glue moss to the lower right corner of the arch as shown. Cut the roses, statice and gypsophilia into 2"–2½" sprigs and glue among the leaves as shown.

4 Push the dowel into one foam ball; remove, apply glue and reinsert. Mark a ¾" circle on the back of the ball. Glue dried rosebuds to cover the ball leaving the circle bare. When the glue is dry use tweezers or toothpicks to pick up small pieces of moss and push them in between the buds. Glue moss into the empty circle. Push the remaining foam ball into the pot, secure with glue. Glue moss on top. Push the other end of the dowel into the foam in the pot; remove, apply glue and reinsert. Run a 7" wire length through the hole in the bottom of the pot and out the top back. Wire the pot to the right side of the arch as shown in the large photo.

20" lacquered grapevine wreath
2 stems of silk burgundy watsonia
6 stems of dark red morning dew silk roses, each with one 3" wide blossom and six 3" long leaves
2 oz. of white dried ti tree
2 oz. of dark red stem-dyed dried caspia
2 yards of 1½" wide magenta organza ribbon
1 yard of 1½" wide pink organza ribbon
U-shaped floral pins
1 oz. of Spanish moss
4"x2"x3" piece of floral foam for drieds
basic supplies (see inside the front cover)

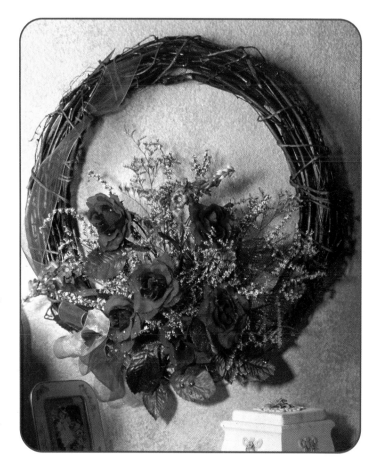

1 Cut the foam to fit inside the bottom curve of the wreath; glue in place. Cover the front of the foam with moss and secure with U-shaped floral pins. Wire the foam to the wreath for extra strength.

2 Use the magenta ribbon to make a center loop and the first two 3" loops of a puffy bow (see inside the back cover). Lay pink ribbon on top of the magenta and hold them together to make four 4" loops ending with one 22" magenta tail. Glue the bow at 7:00. Loop and glue the tail up the left side of the wreath.

3 Cut the ti tree into 6½"–9" sprigs and attach three 9" sprigs to wood picks (see inside the front cover). Insert the picks into the foam in a fan arrangement; save the remaining ti tree for step 4. Cut the rose stems to the following lengths: one 8", one 7", one 5", two 3" and one 1" long. Glue the 8" and 7" stems to the right and left of the foam center. Glue the 5" stem into the front just left of center. Glue the 3" stems on each side of the 5" stem extending out from the center. Glue the 1" stem at the center bottom. Remove the leaves from the remaining stems and glue among the lower roses to fill empty spaces.

4 Cut the watsonia into two 9" and two 8" sprigs. Insert one 9" sprig at the center back of the arrangement curving the flower to the right. Insert an 8" sprig on each side of the center rose, extending outward. Glue the last sprig into the lower right of the arrangement, curving up the side of the wreath. Cut the caspia into 4½"–8" sprigs. Insert the longer sprigs at the back of the arrangement and the shorter sprigs among the roses and watsonia. Fill in with the remaining 6½" ti tree. Attach a wire hanger to the wreath back.

back view

1

2

3

4

Vine Heart Wreath

10"x10" grapevine heart with 15" tails
3 stems of mauve silk roses, each with one 2" wide
    blossom, one ¾" wide open bud and many 1½" long
    leaves
1 stem of mauve silk roses with fourteen ½"–¾" wide
    blossoms and buds
1 stem of ½" wide light pink silk wildflowers with
    many clusters of four ½" wide blossoms
1 oz. of dried lavender
1 oz. of rose peppergrass
2½ yards of 1⅜" wide green/mauve/ombre wire-edged
    ribbon
basic supplies (see inside the front cover)

1 Cut a 12" ribbon length and set it aside. Use the remaining ribbon to make an oblong bow (see inside the back cover) with a center loop, two 2½" loops, six 3" loops and one 22" tail. Glue the bow to the upper left heart with the tail extending through the center and behind the bottom point of the heart. Glue one end of the 12" length to the bottom point of the heart and weave it through the right tails of the heart as shown.

2 Cut the 2" roses off the stems. Glue one directly below the bow, one at the bottom point of the heart and the third between the first two. Remove the leaves from these stems and glue them evenly spaced among the roses.

3 Cut the small roses and buds with 1"–2" stems; glue in clusters of 2–4 to the right of the bow and below each 2" rose. Cut the stems of the wildflower clusters to 1". Glue among the roses individually and in clusters of 3–4.

4 Cut the lavender and peppergrass to 2"–3" and glue evenly spaced among the bow loops and blossoms as shown in the large photo. Attach a wire hanger (see inside the front cover) to the heart back.

Rustic Window

7"x9" wood window frame with a ledge
one 3" wide dried blue hydrangea blossom head
five 1" long sprigs of mauve dried peppergrass
four 1" long sprigs of dried silver king artemesia
three 9" long birch or grapevine twigs
2¼"x2" wood birdhouse
wood cutouts: 1½" wide blue bird, 1¾" long red
    heart, 2"x¾" brown sign with "All Birdies
    Welcome" written in black
blue/white checked fabric: two 6½"x4" and two
    ⅜"x3" pieces
small handful of Spanish moss, 2" tuft of sheet moss
1½"x¼" piece of tree bark
acrylic paints: dark brown, light brown, medium blue,
    dark blue, white
crackle medium
walnut gel stain, soft cloth
paintbrushes: #1 liner brush, #10 and #4 flat shaders
small sea sponge
1¾" sawtooth hanger with tacks, hammer
basic supplies (see inside the front cover)

1 Use the #10 brush to paint the window frame dark blue and let dry. Paint it with crackle medium, following the manufacturer's instructions; let dry. Paint the frame white and let dry. Attach the hanger to the top back of the frame.

2 **Curtains:** Place the 6½"x4" fabric pieces side by side and round each inside bottom corner (see diagram). Apply a line of glue along the top back of the frame. Pleat the top edges of each fabric piece while pressing them into the glue. **Tiebacks:** Wrap a 3" fabric strip around each curtain below the frame crosspiece. Glue the ends to the frame back.

3 Apply a coat of stain to the sign, heart and bird. Wipe off with the cloth. Glue the sign as shown and ½" tufts of Spanish moss around the sign. Glue the twig to the left of the frame and the bird to the twig. Glue the heart and a 1" tuft of moss at the base of the twigs.

4 Use the #4 brush to paint the birdhouse light brown and the roof medium blue. Use the liner to outline the door and windows with dark brown. Sponge the roof (see inside the front cover) with dark blue then white. Apply stain to the entire bird house and wipe off with the cloth. Glue the house to the right window ledge and sheet moss around the base. Glue the bark to the center ledge. Break the hydrangea blossom head into 2–3 blossom sprigs. Glue the sprigs around the birdhouse and across the window ledge.

Woodland Home

18" round grapevine wreath
6½"x4½" birdhouse with 2" long hanger
2 yards of 2½" wide dark red checked wire-edged
 ribbon
one 2½" long blue mushroom bird
1 stem of dark red silk dogwood with two 3", four
 2½", five 2", six 1½" wide blossoms and 4 buds
1 oz. of dried German statice
4 oz. of green preserved eucalyptus
1 oz. of burgundy dried wild oats
nine 18" strands of raffia
2" ball of Spanish moss
1 oz. of green sheet moss
handful of reindeer moss
basic supplies (see inside the front cover)

1 Wire the birdhouse to the inside bottom of the wreath. Spread and glue a 3" tuft of sheet moss over right side of the roof, a 4" tuft on the wreath just to the right of the house, a 2" tuft 4" to the left of the house. Glue tufts of reindeer moss around the base of the birdhouse to cover the wire. Glue the Spanish moss into the house opening.

2 Use the ribbon to make an oblong bow (see inside the back cover) with a center loop, two 4" loops, four 4½" loops and 7" tails. Hold three raffia strands together and make a 2½" loop with a 10" tail; wire to secure; repeat. Glue one on each side of the bow's center loop. Use your thumbnail to shred the raffia into thin strands. Glue the bow at the right top of the wreath as shown. Cut the eucalyptus into 5"–6"

sprigs. Beginning just left of the bow, glue the eucalyptus to the wreath front, extending downward and ending 6" beyond the birdhouse.

3 Use the remaining raffia to make a shoestring bow with 2" loops and 6" tails. Glue the bow to the wreath 4" to the left of the house. Glue the bird to the moss above the bow.

4 Cut the dogwood into 2"–5" single-flower sprigs. Glue two 2" and two 1½" blossoms to the right of the upper bow. Glue the remaining dogwood evenly throughout the eucalyptus as shown in the large photo. Cut the statice and wild oats into 4" sprigs and glue evenly spaced among the eucalyptus and dogwood. Attach a wire hanger to the wreath back.

Teasel & Eucalyptus Crown

33"x12" crown arch

4 oz. of green preserved eucalyptus

8 stems of burgundy dried teasel

1 oz. of blue dried wild oats

2 oz. of white dried ti tree

2 oz. of burgundy dried stem-dyed caspia

2½ yards of 3" wide burgundy mesh ribbon

2½ yards of 1⅞" wide burgundy/blue heart print ribbon

basic supplies (see inside the front cover)

1 Cut the eucalyptus stems to 11"–15" and glue to the center bottom of the crown extending upward and outward in a fan shape.

2 Cut the teasel to the following lengths: two 13", three 10", two 8" and one 5". Glue the 13" stems to the crown base, one extending toward each end. Refer to the photo to glue the remaining teasel stems among the eucalyptus.

3 Cut the ti tree and oats into 6"–9" sprigs and the caspia into 8"–15" sprigs. Glue them evenly spaced throughout the eucalyptus, with some on top of the eucalyptus and some tucked in behind, adding depth. Glue shorter sprigs close to the center of the fan arrangement and longer sprigs lower in the arrangement.

4 Lay the heart ribbon on the mesh ribbon and handle as one to make a puffy bow (see inside the back cover) with a center loop, eight 4" loops and 9" tails. Glue the bow to the center bottom. Attach a wire hanger to the crown back.

four 6" wide blue dried
    hydrangea heads
2 oz. of dried silver king
    artemesia
2 oz. of dried caspia
8 oz. of 36" long raffia strands
6 yards of 3" wide blue twisted
    paper ribbon
basic supplies (see inside the
    front cover)

1 Untwist the paper ribbon and cut a 30" length. Cut this piece in half lengthwise. Set aside forty-four strands of raffia and separate the remainder into two equal bunches. Separate one bunch of raffia into three equal portions, place one strip of ribbon on the center portion and wire the upper ends together. Braid for 30" and wire the lower ends to secure. Repeat for another braid. Lay the two braids in a straight line overlapping the ends 7". Wire together in three places and form the center wire into a hanging loop.

2 Fold the lower ends of each braid under and secure with wire. For each end: Hold ten raffia strands together and make a shoestring bow (see inside the back cover) with 3" loops and 12"–14" tails. Shred the raffia into thin strands with your thumbnail. Glue the bow to one end of the braid. Repeat for the other end. Cut six 24" raffia lengths and use each to make a shoestring bow with 2½" loops and 7" tails. Glue three bows 7" apart on each braid half as shown in the large photo.

3 Separate the hydrangea heads into 3" wide clusters. Glue one into the center of each end bow and the rest evenly spaced along the braids. Cut the caspia and artemesia into 4"–6" sprigs. Glue them evenly around the hydrangea clusters as shown.

4 Use the remaining paper ribbon to make a puffy bow with a center loop, ten 4½" loops and 6" tails. Cut the ends in an inverted "V" then glue the bow to the center of the swag. Form a raffia strand into six 3½" loops; wire the ends. Repeat to make a total of nine loop clusters. Glue them evenly among the bow loops. Cut the remaining raffia strands to 22", fold in half and wire together at the fold. Glue under the center loop of the ribbon bow. Shred the tails with your thumbnail. Attach a wire hanger to the swag ends.

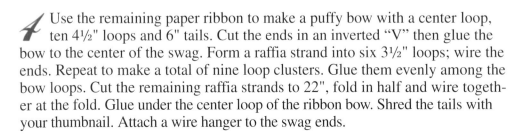

16" tall twig trellis
24" long silk leaf garland with 1"–2" long white-spotted green leaves
one 6" wide blue dried hydrangea blossom head
1 stem of mauve silk delphinium with many ½"–¾" wide blossoms
four 1" sprigs of mauve dried statice
3 stems of blue silk mums, each with one 1½" wide blossom and one 2" long leaf
one 2½"x2¼" terra cotta pot
acrylic whitewash spray paint
4½"x3" seed packet (of your choice)
handful of sheet moss
2" tuft of Spanish moss
1¼"x1½" blue resin butterfly
2" square of floral foam for drieds
U-shaped floral pins
basic supplies (see inside the front cover)

1 Spray the trellis lightly with whitewash and let dry. Glue the pot angled as shown, 4" above the bottom of the trellis, and secure with wire. Glue the foam into the pot; cover with Spanish moss and secure with U-shaped floral pins. Glue the sheet moss around the base of the pot and near the bottom of the trellis.

2 Glue the seed packet at an angle, 1" above the flower pot. Cut the garland into two 12" lengths. Glue each length behind the pot and wire up the trellis as shown.

3 Cut the hydrangea into four 2" and one 1" wide clusters. Glue a 2" cluster under the pot, one in the pot and one to each garland length above the seed packet. Glue the 1" cluster at the top right. Cut the delphinium stem to 8" and wire behind the seed packet angling up to the top left side of the trellis.

4 Glue three statice sprigs into the pot and one below the lowest hydrangea. Cut the mum stems to 2" and insert into the pot. Glue the butterfly to the trellis over the mums as shown.

Spirea Spray

28"x18" S-shaped twig swag

1 stem of white latex spirea with one 14" and one 16" sprig of many 1" wide blossom clusters and 1¾" long leaves

2 stems of yellow silk statice, each with four 3" wide clusters of ½" wide blossoms

1 oz. of dried bromus secalinus

1 oz. of green dried sweet Annie

2⅔ yards of 1⅞" wide white/pink/green print ribbon

basic supplies (see inside the front cover)

1 Use two yards of ribbon to make an oblong bow (see inside the back cover) with a center loop, two 3" loops, six 3½" loops and 5" tails. Set the remaining ribbon aside for step 3. Glue the bow to the center of the swag. Cut one spirea sprig to 11" and one to 15". Wire the 11" sprig to extend from below the bow curving down the swag. Wire the 15" sprig up the swag, starting 3" above the bow.

2 Cut the statice clusters off the stems and glue four evenly spaced above and three below the bow. Cut the last cluster into smaller pieces and glue them evenly among the leaves, filling empty spaces.

3 Cut the remaining ribbon in half and make a 3" loop with a 4½" tail from each piece; wire to secure. Glue one loop underneath the statice and leaves 6" from each end of the swag.

4 Cut the bromus into 4"–5" sprigs and glue in clusters of 3–4 sprigs among the leaves and bow loops. Cut the sweet Annie into 5"–6" sprigs and glue single sprigs evenly spaced throughout the materials as shown.

Victorian Watering Can

5¾"x5"x3½" wire watering can

five stems of cream dried-look silk rosebuds,
   each with a ½" wide blossom

2 oz. of dried caspia

1 oz. of dried nigella

½ oz. of dried mini gypsophila

3 oz. of dried pink peppergrass

1 oz. of green dried plumosus fern

3 stems of dried burgundy strawflowers, each
   with a 2" wide blossom

½ oz. each of dried purple and white statice

½ oz. of dried pink globe amaranth

2 yards of 1½" wide pink mesh ribbon

4"x4"x8" block of floral foam for drieds

3 oz. sheet moss

U-shaped floral pins

basic supplies (see inside the front cover)

1 Cut the foam to fit the watering can, allowing enough room for a layer of moss around it. Use U-shaped floral pins to attach the moss to the foam. Apply glue to the back and bottom of the foam and insert it into the watering can.

2 Cut the roses into one 10", two 8", and two 6" stems. Cut one strawflower to 9", one to 7", and one to 6". Glue the roses and strawflowers into the foam in a fan, positioning them as shown.

3 Cut the peppergrass into 5"–11" sprigs and the caspia and mini gypsophila into 5"–10" sprigs. Insert them among the roses and strawflowers, near flowers of similar heights at the same angles.

4 Use the ribbon to make a puffy bow (see inside the back cover) with a center loop, six 2½" loops, one 6" tail and one 8" tail. Glue the bow to the top right of the can near the handle. Loop and glue the tails across the front as shown in the large photo. Cut the statice, globe amaranth and nigella into 5"–8" sprigs; insert evenly spaced near materials of similar lengths. Repeat with the fern.

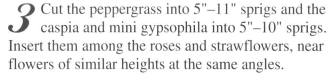

Shades of Fall Wreath

22" wispy vine sunburst wreath
2 oz. of dried wheat
1 oz. of bleached dried rattail grass
1 oz. of rust dried poa grass
2 oz. of rust dried oats
1 oz. of green dried sweet Annie
2 oz. of mini gypsophila
1½ yards of 2½" wide rust/green/tan fall
   print ribbon
basic supplies (see inside the front cover)

1 Use the ribbon to make an oblong bow (see inside the back cover) with a center loop, two 3" and two 3½" loops and 7½" tails. Glue the bow to the wreath at 7:00.

2 Make a cluster of four 3"–9" sprigs each of wheat, rattail, poa and oats. Hold in a bunch, wire the base and glue behind the bow, angling upward.

3 Cut the stems of the remaining wheat to 1". Glue them around the wreath following the lines of the sunburst, placing some near the center and other pieces towards the outer ends as shown.

4 Cut and glue stems of rattail, poa and oats as for the wheat. Cut the gypsophila and sweet Annie into 1½" sprigs; glue in and around the bow and around the center of the wreath as shown in the large photo.

Harvest Time Wheelbarrow

11"x5"x6" wooden wheelbarrow
2 oz. of dried bromus secalinus
2 oz. of rust dried campo flowers
1 oz. of rust dried poa grass
1 silk fall leaf candle ring with six clusters
    of many 1" long orange/yellow leaves
four 18" long strands of raffia
one 4" tall scarecrow
1 artificial pumpkin pick with five 1" wide
    orange pumpkins
2 artificial corn picks with three 1½" long ears
    of brown, orange and yellow corn
4"x3½ "x2¾" block of floral foam for drieds
handful of Spanish moss
U-shaped floral pins
3" wired wood picks
wood-tone spray paint
basic supplies (see inside the front cover)

1 Cut the foam to fit in the wheelbarrow and to extend ½" above rim. Glue it in place, cover with Spanish moss and secure with U-shaped floral pins. hold the raffia strands together and make a shoestring bow (see inside the back cover) with seven 1½" loops and 4"–5" tails. Shred the raffia loops and tails with your thumbnail. Wrap the wire of a floral pick around the bow center and insert the pick into the foam at the front left corner of the wheelbarrow.

2 Cut three pumpkins off the pick and glue behind the bow to the right. Cut the stems of the corn picks to 2" and glue one on each side of the pumpkins. Glue two pumpkins behind the left corn. Glue two wood picks to the back of the scarecrow's legs extending 1" below his feet. Glue him behind the pumpkins.

3 Spray the leaves with the wood-tone paint to darken them; let dry. Cut the leaf clusters off the candle ring. Insert one on each side of the bow, and three behind the scarcrow as shown. Glue the last cluster to the outside front of the wheelbarrow.

4 Cut the stems of the campo flowers to 3½"–4". Attach to picks (see inside the front cover) in clusters of 8–12. Insert evenly spaced throughout the arrangement. Cut the bromus to 4"–5", attach to wood picks in clusters of 3–4 and insert evenly spaced into the foam extending outward. Cut poa stems to 2"–5" and insert evenly spaced among materials of similar lengths.

14"x14" wicker and iron sleigh
6 stems of green vinyl evergreen, each with five 10"
   long sprigs
3 stems of wide dark red silk poinsettias, each with a
   2½" wide blossom, and one with a 2" long leaf
1 oz. of dark red dried cockscomb
1 oz. of dark red dried rice flowers
1 oz. of dried German statice
½ oz. of yellow dried mini gypsophila
two 2" long pine cones
2 yards of 2¼" wide wired gold mesh holiday ribbon
1¼ yards of ½" wide gold cord
gold spray paint
1 strand of 35 clear Christmas lights
one 4" wide gold glittered plastic snowflake
4"x4"x8" block of floral foam for drieds
1 oz. of Spanish moss
old newspapers
3" wired wood picks
basic supplies (see inside the front cover)

1 Cut the foam to fit in the sleigh, leaving a ½"
space around the foam; glue in place. Tuck the
moss between the foam and the sides of the sleigh.
Cut the evergreen stems to 12" and insert evenly
spaced into the foam, shaping the sprigs to extend over
the sides of the sleigh. String lights throughout the
branches with the plug extending out the back of the
sleigh.

2 Cut a 30" length of gold cord and make a shoestring bow (see inside the back cover) with two 3"
loops, one 8" tail and one 5" tail. Knot the end of each
tail and glue the bow into the branches in the front
right corner of the sleigh. Lay the pine cones on newspapers and spray them gold. Let dry. Attach each to a
wood pick (see inside the front cover) and insert them
near the center of the sleigh toward the back. Use the
ribbon to make a puffy bow with a center loop, six
3½" loops, one 7" tail and one 14" tail. Glue the bow
to a branch near the back of the sleigh. Weave the long
tail down through the branches to the front of the
sleigh and curve the short tail up and out the back corner of the sleigh. Glue the remaining length of gold
cord underneath the loop of the bow and weave the
cord down through the branches. Glue the other end
behind the knot of the shoestring bow at the front of
the sleigh.

3 Glue the snowflake at an angle between the pine
cones. Insert two poinsettas in front of the
snowflake and the third one with leaf in the greenery
2" in front of the puffy bow.

4 Separate the cockscomb into 1"–2" wide clusters
and the rice flowers into 2" lengths and glue
throughout the greens. Cut the statice and gypsophila into
3" sprigs and glue throughout the arrangement.